Happy & Healtl

A Guide for Parents

Advice, hints and tips from expert child-psychologist Dr Janet Hall PhD

hinkler

Ready to Go!

Happy & Healthy Habits

A Guide for Parents

Advice, hints and tips from expert child-psychologist
Dr Janet Hall PhD

hinkler

Published by Hinkler Books Pty Ltd
45–55 Fairchild Street
Heatherton Victoria 3202 Australia
www.hinkler.com

hinkler

© Hinkler Books Pty Ltd 2018

Author: Dr Janet Hall
Reward-chart System Content: Kylie Appel
Cover Design: Sam Grimmer
Internal Design: Hinkler Design Studio
Illustration: Alison Brown
Prepress: Graphic Print Group

ISBN: 978 1 4889 0948 1

Printed and bound in China

Contents

Introduction 5

Reward Charts 6

About this Guide 13

How Children Learn 14

Improving and Looking After Myself 24

Eating, Sleeping and Healthy Self-care 32

Rewards Guide 41

Top Parenting Tips to Remember 48

Introduction

It is important to focus on creating healthy habits early. This creates a solid foundation of physical and mental health that allows children to access their internal resources to change any unhealthy habits they may have slipped into as they mature. These resources can include patience, energy, focus, motivation and confidence, which should all be modelled by the parents.

Also, this kit will help your family initiate and maintain good habits through positive reinforcement, and implicitly to stop bad habits by substituting then for these better actions and behaviour.

Habits are built through routines, which depend on an adult setting up a program to suit the family. Parents need to:

- Be excellent time-keepers.
- Shop for healthy food and make mealtimes consistent.
- Set realistic bedtimes according to a child's age. Busy children need more than enough sleep if they are to wake each day feeling positive and energised.
- Set a family outdoor activity each weekend.

A challenging habit to teach children is restricting the time spent on electronic devices and television. Over-exposure to screens can cause:

- Behavioural difficulties, including emotional and social problems.
- Being overweight and sluggish.
- Irregular sleep, trouble falling asleep and resisting bedtime.
- Less time to play.

Habits are hard to break. The sooner in life we build good, healthy habits, the easier it is to keep them. When good habits are in place, it's easier to resist bad ones.

Reward Charts

As parents, you juggle work, school, family commitments and many other things. This reward chart with stickers helps busy families connect with each other in a fun and meaningful way, makes life easier and helps you get the most out of family time.

There are many benefits to using reward charts as a parenting strategy:

- Reward charts are the perfect tool for helping promote good behaviour, habits and attitudes in children, as well as discouraging and changing bad behaviour.

- Reward charts are a way to introduce, encourage and reinforce new skills and knowledge.

- Parents can be encouraged by seeing clearly their child's progress and many occurrences of good behaviour, as well as easily spotting areas to work on together.

- Reward charts encourage responsibility, self-confidence and self-reliance in children.

- Positive-based teaching has been widely demonstrated to be much more effective in moderating children's behaviour and having happy and healthy outcomes for all involved, as will be explored more through this instructional guide.

- Reward charts involve active engagement and participation of both parents or guardians and children and are a positive and fun experience.

About the *Ready to Go* Reward Chart and Stickers

The *Happy & Healthy Habits* kit contains the following components:

A reward chart

A certificate of achievement

20 goal stickers

70 motivational stickers

20 reward stickers

10 blank reward stickers and 10 blank goal stickers

Reward Chart

Featuring fun, appealing illustrations, the reward chart allows you to set goals, monitor progress and reward achievements.

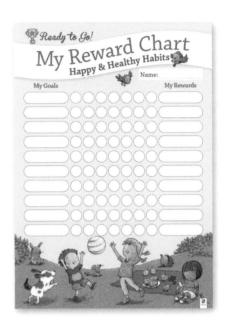

Goal Stickers

These carefully devised goals allow you to tailor your chart to suit your child's age and their developmental stage. The goal stickers are designed to encourage healthy habits, make chores more appealing, instil a sense of responsibility and independence and develop positive values and morals. You can also update goals according to your child's ever-evolving requirements. Once you have chosen a goal, explain it clearly to your child. Remember, too many goals at one time will be confusing, so try not to choose more than ten. Also, be patient, as it takes time for kids to learn new ways of behaving.

Motivational Stickers

We all like receiving praise. And as a child is developing their self-esteem and how they feel about themselves, they thrive on praise even more than we do. Praising positive behaviour also increases the chance that behaviour will be repeated. These offer your child instant recognition and encouragement for a goal achieved or a job well done. Once they achieve a set task or goal, praise their behaviour and select an appropriate motivational sticker to add to the chart.

Reward Stickers

These give your child an end goal. A reward can be chosen once your child has received seven motivational stickers, or you can select the reward before they start to add extra incentive. This kit features over 40 reward suggestions that are inexpensive and fun for the whole family. The suggested rewards are not only things that contemporary kids and families will enjoy, but will also encourage good habits, such as a family picnic where kids can be active outdoors and eat healthy food.

My reward is to:
Buy Seeds to Sprout

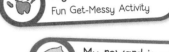

My reward is a:
Fun Get-Messy Activity

My reward is a:
Sleepover

Blank Customisable Stickers

Use the additional blank stickers to personalise your child's own goals and rewards. You can use a whiteboard marker to write on and wipe off the rewards.

My goal is to:
....

My reward is:
....

Certificate of Completion

Use the completion certificate as an achievement award once your child completes their *Ready to Go* reward chart.

How to Use the Stickers and Reward Chart

Step 1 – Choose Your Goals

Select goals with your child. Explain the goal clearly then stick it to your Smart Chart. Remember you can make your own goals using the blank stickers.

TOP TIP
Too many goals at one time can be confusing for little ones, so try not to choose more than five at a time for the under 5-year-olds and keep adding more for the 5–10-year-olds as required.

My goal is to:
Do Things for Myself

My goal is to:
Choose Healthy Snacks

My goal is to:
Use the Toilet

Step 2 – Choose Your Rewards

Select rewards together with your child to suit their individual interests. Remember, you can make your own rewards using the blank stickers.

TOP TIP
Choosing rewards before your child starts can add extra incentive. Encourage your child to develop their own interests and feel a sense of ownership about choosing their reward. Sometime, however, a mystery reward or one they feel like at the time can keep things fresh.

My reward is a:
Play Date

My reward is to:
Go for a Bike Ride

My reward is a:
Fun Arty, Crafty Activity

Step 3 – Choose a Motivational Sticker

When your child achieves a goal, praise their behaviour and select a motivational sticker to stick to your reward chart.

TOP TIP
Praise the little changes and successes. Don't wait until your child does something perfectly before you offer a compliment. Describe exactly what you are happy about, like the way they shared and played nicely.

Step 4 – Redeem Your Rewards

When your child has completed their weekly goals and has received all seven motivational stickers, they can collect and redeem their rewards. Woohoo! It may be a good idea to take pictures of your child enjoying their reward to use as extra incentive for next time.

TOP TIP
Rewards can be used to bring everyone in the family together in a fun and meaningful way.

Step 5 – Present Your Certificate

Present the certificate to your child once they have filled in the whole reward chart. Congratulating a child for a job well done is a way to motivate them and recognise their efforts. Make a big deal when presenting it to your child. Children thrive on praise and it makes them feel special.

Tips to Help Your Child

As you use the stickers and reward chart, try to keep the following tips in mind. They'll help your child feel good and encourage them to work towards achieving their goals.

- Try to offer your child some words of encouragement every day.

- Describe exactly what you are happy about. Instead of just telling them that they're good, tell them why they're good. Say exactly what you are happy with, such as the way they played nicely with a friend and shared well.

- Don't compliment by comparing one child to another. This often creates feelings of resentment.

- Try to praise good behaviour instead of criticising bad. It takes a lot of praise to outweigh one criticism.

- Praise the little changes and successes. Don't wait until they do something perfectly before you offer a compliment.

- Encourage each child to develop their own interests. Let your child feel a sense of pride about being different.

About this Guide

We all want the very best for our children and the *Ready to Go* parent guide can help achieve this by providing a dynamic and rewarding parenting information resource for you to share with the whole family.

This guide contains helpful hints and tips for each suggested goal and reward in this kit, creating fun ways to help kids reach their full potential.

The guide also features:

- parenting advice on child development and how children learn
- information on modelling best behaviours for children
- tips for establishing rules and routines
- applying consequences for behaviour, including a discussion of rewards and punishment
- strategies for parenting with compassion and understanding.

The *Ready to Go* parent guide also features specific parenting advice on a selection of topics included in the reward charts, and includes strategies and techniques that can help address specific behaviours and that can also be applied to more general behaviours and conduct.

How Children Learn

To get the best results not only from this reward chart but also more generally for raising children, it helps to know how children learn. Factors influencing how children learn behaviours include the **4 'C's:**

1. Copying: parents must model best behaviours for children.

2. Cues: these are signals, reminders, arrangements, rules and routines.

3. Consequences: these are rewards and punishment.

4. Compassion: parents must balance the above three 'C's with still being caring and understanding.

There's a short summary of each of these 'C's below and then the following pages have some guidelines for each in depth as they are an excellent and comprehensive way for parents and guardians to teach their children to build their best behaviour.

1. Copying: parents need to model best behaviour for children to copy

Parenting is often modelled from what our parents did to us and children similarly pick up on their parents' or guardians' own behaviours. They also pick things up from TV, magazines, books and other media.

Increasingly this also includes what children may see online, so it's always important to consider carefully what children are exposed to and absorbing and make sure it's suitable. Sometimes just providing commentary on what they are reading or watching can be effective in showing what behaviours are suitable and which are not.

2. Cues: signals, reminders, arrangements, rules and routines

We learn by doing what we are told and then getting into good habits which are both consciously and unconsciously repeated. This consistent repeating of actions is triggered by reminders, signals, arrangements, routines and agreements.

These can come from different sources: we draw from the memories of our own childhood experiences with our families, from contemporary guidelines from different media and we create our own rules and rituals to suit our particular family.

3. Consequences: reward and punishment

Generally speaking, if you reward a behaviour it will increase. If you punish a behaviour it will decrease. The type of consequences that our parents applied (rewards or punishments) may have been inconsistently imposed, depending very much on their mood at the time. It's important to try and be as consistent as possible, as you don't want to be sending mixed messages.

4. Compassion: being understood and listened to equals caring communication

While the three 'C's above are all vital, so is remembering that kids are not perfect and have a lot to learn and remember and that everyone has challenging days. Remember to always be patient, loving and understanding and listen to what your children have to say.

Copying

You are your child's most significant role model. You must be the person you want your child to be. This means that you should always endeavour to:

- Be polite
- Control your bad moods (don't overreact)
- Tell the truth
- Keep your sense of humour
- Be resilient (bounce back with a positive attitude after adversity)
- Choose your friends wisely and maintain good relationships
- Keep your space clean
- Keep your life organised
- Stay fit and healthy.

Children, like adults, learn from what they see other people do. Modelling comes from things that we read, things that we watch on television or on the Internet and things that we see others do or hear others say. We don't necessarily have to have these experiences ourselves.

Children who observe adults using bad manners are likely to copy these behaviours. To be a good role model, say please and thank you, admit your mistakes, apologise and treat people with kindness and respect.

Cues

The key strategy to preventing child behavioural problems is to implement the **4 'R's:**

1. Rules

2. Regulations

3. Routines

4. Rituals.

Just watch children meet: they don't even need to know each other's names, but they immediately select roles and rules. For example, if they are playing a game about a pirate ship, they might say, 'You're the first mate, I'm the captain and these are the rules!'

- When giving orders and setting rules for your child, you should allow them to be carried out independently, but intervene or provide help under the following circumstances:

- When you feel your child may be in danger

- When you know for sure your child cannot handle the situation or problem by themselves.

Unclear Rules Or Routines

Children often fight over 'whose turn is it?'. Fighting can reach fever pitch in no time at all when emotions are involved, especially when kids think something is unfair.

Children may dispute parents' rules but they do respect the system of rules. Rules are the roadmaps to communication because they establish agreements. Children need to grasp the fundamental importance of keeping agreements if they are to become responsible adults.

There are a few very important guidelines for creating rules:

- Keep the rules short and simple: what is wanted and for when.

- Phrase the rules in a positive tone. State what you want your child to do, not what you don't want them to do.

- Post the rules early to avoid disputes. The best and most convenient place to post the rules is the greatest art gallery in the world: the family refrigerator!

- Create the rules together with the children: don't dictate!

The reward chart is the perfect way to establish new rules, make sure they're clear, encourage children to follow them and allow them to track their process.

Rules can help prevent fights. If you are in doubt as to whether a rule is necessary, just look for the moments of hottest dispute. That's when rules can prevent problems!

Explaining New Rules

Because rules apply according to the chronological age and maturity of your children, it is important that parents clearly communicate rule changes or developments. The transition from being 'mummy's/daddy's little helper' to being a person with regular domestic chores may not be easily digestible. Once you have your rules and requirements you need to make them very specific so there can never be a dispute about the expected standards.

Consequences

Parenting power comes from careful use of consequences. Most parents think that they do a good job of rewarding children most of the time. Parents are usually reluctant to punish their children, reserving punishment for dangerous or decidedly naughty behaviours.

Most parents do not know the truth about rewards and punishments. All behaviour has a payoff:

- Rewards increase behaviour: people keep doing things that make them feel better.
- Punishments decrease behaviour: people stop doing things that don't make them feel better or that make them feel worse. This may not naturally happen as a result of their action, so may need to happen as a result of punishment for that action.

Rewards

When rewarding children, remember: a reward is only a reward if it increases a behaviour. Ask your child what they would work for, compromise on, be willing to do, or suffer with, in order to have what they want. Then, you can identify immediately if a reward really is a reward by observing whether the behaviour you were rewarding increases.

Some parents are actually rewarding children when they think they are punishing them. If you think that you are punishing a child with something you think they don't like, check to see if it is a punishment by observing whether that behaviour decreases. Some types of perceived punishment can in fact be a reward when it gives a child attention, as attention can be rewarding.

Rewards work best when they are applied consistently and follow immediately after the behaviour that you want to increase.

Try the 'rather' rule: Use things that children like to do as a reward for things they don't like to do. For example, a child who'd 'rather' watch TV needs to be reminded that he or she is not able to watch TV unless their room is clean. The TV (liked) is the reward for the clean room (disliked).

Visual Tracking Rewards

Children may all vary in their choice of what they find rewarding, but most seem to enjoy visual tracking rewards, like the reward chart and stickers in this kit. Parents can use this strategy to encourage children to have fight-free and yell-free days.

Parents can also challenge themselves to join in and have their own chart for various behaviours they would like to increase in themselves. This could be in their roles as parents, for instance having a nag-free day or spending some quality time with their children, or personal health and fitness goals. There is nothing to stop these goals and motivating rewards going up on the family reward chart, so that the family can all feel in it together!

Punishment

Every time you punish your child, you are modelling modes of punishment and it's likely that your child will learn from this model. Some types of punishment can lead to fear, resentment and escape.

Types of punishment include:

- Withdrawal of a positive: including taking away TV privileges, made to go to bed early, being grounded, not being able to see their friends, not having treats, or having a time out.

- Verbal punishment: including criticism, labelling, nagging or ridicule. Some tones of voice can also be punishing, for example screaming, groaning, threatening, sarcasm, lecturing or swearing.

- Physical punishment: including anything that physically hurts the child, such as smacking.

Parents who punish often believe that it is working because they temporarily get the child to stop the behaviour. However, parents may observe that over a period of time the misbehaviour is not decreasing. The punishment is only temporarily effective.

Applying punishment puts both you and your child at risk of hurting and being hurt, and you may still not achieve the result that you wanted. For all these reasons, rewards are always more attractive than punishment. If you do use punishment, be realistic, be aware and beware.

When is punishment necessary? There are some times when punishment can be necessary and appropriate. These are:

- When the behaviour is dangerous or life-threatening and has to stop.
- When there is a total 'no win' situation for both parties and new behaviour has to begin somehow.

Time outs are recommended forms of punishment, if it's absolutely necessary.

Time Outs

The time-out technique is sometimes misunderstood. It really means time out from positive reinforcement; that is, not being allowed to have anything positive or rewarding happen to or around your child.

Find a spot in the house that doesn't contain fun things for the child to do. The child must be small enough to go to the time out space without a physical fight. The child should be compliant enough to stay until given permission to leave. Never lock your child in a room.

To make time out work:

1. The instant your child begins a tantrum, say 'Time out' and take your child to the time-out spot.
2. Make no other comment.
3. Take the child to time out every time the behaviour occurs. A good rule of thumb is number of minutes per age (i.e. two minutes for two-year-olds, six minutes for six-year-olds).
4. Let the child come out. If the child is still having a tantrum, extend the time-out period until it stops.

5. If the tantrum started when you asked the child to do something, repeat the request so that the child does what is asked.

6. Keep repeating as necessary.

Combining Reward and Punishment

Try to combine reward and punishment: reward the good behaviour and ignore the bad behaviour. This is easier said than done.

When you choose to ignore, initially the behaviour may get worse before it gets better. Experts assure us that if you wait, things will improve. Combine rewarding good behaviour with the application of rules and routines and with the removal of rewards or privileges.

Compassion

Children cannot think like adults. It is hard for them to wait; if they want something, they want it NOW! Sometimes neither parents nor children know why they behave badly. They might be:

*   Sick
*   Tired
*   Too young
*   Feeling left out
*   Frightened

Sometimes it's not appropriate for parents to show power and implement consequences. Your child may just need a cuddle and some love. So might you! Use loving firmness: find a balance between clearly allowing consequences to teach life's lessons and being caring and understanding.

Talking with children

Talking with children can be difficult because adults often forget that children are small and a lot of things go over their heads. Remember how you felt as a child: what was important, what wasn't, what you understood, what you didn't, the people you liked, the people you didn't. Sometimes we don't listen to children and instead we talk down to them, we shout, we are too busy or we give them all the answers.

Try these tips:

- When your child wants to talk to you, use cues. Set the scene, turn to face the child and give them all your attention.
- Listen without providing answers, lecturing or criticising.
- Indicate that you are interested and that you would like to hear more.
- Make sure that you are hearing the child by repeating back what you heard but putting it in your own words.

The most important thing parents can give their children is their time. The child needs to feel that the parent is thinking, 'You matter. Your feelings are important to me.' This is why having family-together-time goals and rewards can also be a great idea to help your child feel loved and supported and getting that quality time needed.

Strategy Summary

Here's a summary of this parenting approach, which can be used as a practical strategy to help enforce and measure rules and implement rewards.

Cues to Use

- Use a reward chart
- Create forms and checklists
- Use a timer
- Label items and areas.

Consequences to Use

Positive Consequences:

- Praise
- Lucky dip (of small tokens or toys)
- Visual tracking motivator (like the sticker sheets and reward chart in this kit)
- Special activities (one-on-one time with a parent, playing with a special-occasion toy, etc.).

Negative Consequences:

- Ignore the behaviour
- Remove the object (put the toy away)
- Send child to time out
- Withdraw to your own sanctuary
- Remove privileges: for example, no TV or treats.

Consequences to Avoid

- Name calling, criticising, labelling
- Nagging
- Yelling and screaming
- Hitting and threatening
- Bribes: don't give a reward before the behaviour you desire occurs.

Practising Consistency

- Always do as you say! Otherwise, you will lose credibility and respect and perpetuate your child's bad behaviour.
- Teach your child 'what to do', not 'what not to do'.
- Teach your child to share and cooperate, and reward them for it.
- Use firm consequences early. Avoid the upsets caused by no discipline, no cooperation and frustration.

REMEMBER:
Short-term pain =
Long-term gain

Firm, consistent parenting now will result in responsible children later.

Improving and Looking After Myself

Over time, our daily habits create who we are, so parents have a huge responsibility to teach their children to choose healthy habits. These include habits of daily routine, like eating, sleeping, exercise, and self-care and hygiene. These are the everyday habits that keep us functioning at our best and can also keep us away from the doctor.

This also includes habits of how we think. For instance, parents can teach their children that 'positive thinking may not work every time, but negative thinking DOES'. This encourages children to choose a positive thought when confronted by problem, like 'I can do things if I try my best'.

Improving and looking after yourself also extends to how you conduct yourself around others. Children should understand that when they practise good manners, they are showing that they are respectful and considerate of others' feelings. Teach them that being polite and courteous at mealtimes is important.

Children should learn to:

- Say 'please' and 'thank you'
- Acknowledge when someone is talking
- Wait their turn: be patient when being served or choosing food.

Practise table manners: these include no telling gross jokes, snatching or throwing food, leaning back in chairs, talking with their mouths full, belching loudly or passing wind. Teach your child to say, 'Excuse me' if they burp (and who doesn't?).

At home, it's easy to be a little too relaxed when it comes to table manners. Teach children what is acceptable in public and what isn't, and ensure that you're consistent about the rules. Children find it hard enough to remember household rules: it's even harder to remember different mealtime rules for home and for out.

Goals

These goals are designed to encourage children to improve their skills in looking after themselves. The ten goals in this section are included on the goals stickers and are appropriate for a wide range of ages.

Show Initiative

Give your kids the freedom to come up with their own ways to play, and make sure to praise them for thinking for themselves. Give them the opportunity to have unstructured play: let them make a cubby house, chase bubbles or dance around their rooms if they want to. Initiative may also be shown in the form of helping around the home or reaching for the healthy snack option.

Be Physically Active

Being physically active isn't just fun, it's important to every aspect of a child's development. Whether it's playing inside or outside the home, daily activity helps develop the physical, mental and social skills needed for life. Encourage activities that require some physical activity and join in too!

Read a Book or Join in Story Time

Reading is important for children's language development. It is also a great way to teach them about the world, ignite their imagination and see how others deal with problems and fears. Reading to younger children is just as important. For story time, let your child get involved by getting them to pick the book and encourage them to join in familiar parts of the story.

Have Good Table Manners

For some parents, mealtimes are a bit hard to swallow. Some children make a huge mess when they eat, some won't sit down to eat and others just have poor table manners. Good table manners start before they even get to the table. Establish a good routine by teaching your children to wash their hands before sitting down to the table. Once they're seated, teach them to wait until everyone else is also seated and has been served before they start eating. Also show them it is important to stay in their seats without wiggling in their chairs, going under the table or getting up and down. Encourage your child to sit when they eat, as running around increases chances of choking. Mouths should stay closed

while chewing and pieces should be bite-sized. 'May I please' and 'Thank you' should be used when children would like something, and try to encourage them not to reach across the table. Slurping, burping and squealing are all sounds that should be discouraged. Finally, before getting up at the end of the meal, say, 'May I please be excused?' Try to make mealtime fun. Cut children's food into small potions and serve it on plastic plates, so if they drop their meal it won't make too much mess. And when their manners slip, give them a gentle reminder. And remember, most children don't really understand good manners until they're about five years old.

Limit Screen Time

Television and electronic games present the biggest hurdle to being active. Sitting still for an extended period can mean that children are not getting the active play they need. Try to limit your child's TV and games usage to a certain number of hours per week. Aim for no more than an hour a day of screen time for children aged two to five years old, and set consistent limits for older children.

Look After My Body

Teaching your child to respect their body can start at an early age. It's never too soon to learn about looking after your body. This includes teaching children about personal hygiene, like taking a bath or shower, and brushing their teeth. Exercise is another way to teach them to respect their bodies. It also helps to get plenty of sleep. Of course making healthy food choices is another excellent way to respect their bodies.

Practise Safety Skills

It is important to keep your child physically safe, but it's also critical to teach your child how to keep themselves safe. Teach your child to wear a helmet when riding a bike, not to go off with strangers and to hold hands around cars. Teach them their name, address and phone number and when to call the emergency contact number and what that number is.

Do Things for Myself

Kids love trying to do things without assistance, and being able to do things for themselves is great for a child's self-esteem. Let them get dressed by themselves in the morning or try clearing the table after a meal. Even if you could do it faster, it will help children become independent, self-sufficient and reliable.

Talk About My Feelings

Being able to talk about how they feel will hold your child in great stead. Encourage them to reflect, evaluate, express and articulate their feelings. Spend five minutes each day talking about their day and how they feel about it. Toys, puppets and picture books can be great tools to use to encourage kids to talk about feelings.

Use My Imagination

Using their imagination is fantastic for a child's development. When your child remembers, dreams, creates or improvises, they are developing their problem-solving and creative-thinking skills, as well as entertaining themselves. So, encourage your child to write stories, make plays, paint pictures, play dress-ups and perform puppet shows. Or just have some solo imaginative play.

Suggestions for Blank Goal Stickers

This section contains some ideas for goals about looking after yourself that can be used on the blank goal stickers. These suggestions cover a range of ages, and while some younger children may not be able to do everything needed to achieve a goal in its entirety, they could still be involved in the family's decisions and choices about the goal. You're sure to have some ideas of your own to use on the blank goal stickers too.

> My goal is to:
> Try a New Sport

A child should try many sports, including ones they are not so good at. Trying new things takes kids out of their comfort zones and teaches them many skills. If your child normally plays a team sport, give a more solo sport like swimming or athletics a try, or find a sporting team for them to join if they usually engage in solo activities.

> My goal is to:
> Recycle My Rubbish

Recycling takes some understanding. Explain to your kids which rubbish goes in which bin. It's also a good idea to teach them about composting and recycling plastic bags at the supermarket. They might also enjoy saving old bread to feed to the ducks at the park. Saving cardboard boxes, egg cartons and other materials is also great for craft activities.

> My goal is to: Buy Products
> that are Good for Our Planet

When you take your child shopping and consciously buy eco-friendly products, they learn to recognise environmentally responsible brands. Eco-friendly products may be 100 percent natural, non-toxic, biodegradable, compostable or made from renewable materials. When shopping, let your child choose which products you'll purchase and discuss the environmental benefits of their choice. Look for products that don't over-package, causing more waste.

My goal is to:
Exercise or Play a Sport

Beyond the benefits of exercise, sports teach kids about teamwork, persistence, working towards a goal and learning to deal with failure. Encourage your children to try a variety of sports that require different skills. They can try an activity that requires balance and grace, such as dance and gymnastics. They should also try a sport that requires hand-to-eye coordination, such as cricket or netball, and one that relies on muscular power, like running.

My goal is to:
Have Quiet Time

Quiet time can help children relax and have some time away from stimulation and excitement. It helps children learn how to focus and concentrate. They can spend time alone or with the family, but it should be a period where they are settled and performing a quiet activity. Give kids lots of books to choose from, crayons and paper, building blocks, puzzles or a music player. Avoid screens and the television.

My goal is to:
Take Care of the Environment

There are many ways that children can learn to care for the environment. It could mean putting rubbish in the bin and not littering, being conscious about the importance of not wasting water or planting seeds to grow fresh produce or flowers in the garden.

My goal is to:
Have a Fun Play Time

Playing genuinely helps your child learn. There are many different ways that kids can play, including messy play, active play, word play and pretend play. Remember that play is most valuable when your child is allowed to let their imagination go free.

My goal is to:
Be a Good Sport

Teach children to show good sportsmanship to teammates, opponents, coaches and officials. Try to show your child how to behave with dignity, regardless of if they win or lose a game. Ways of displaying good sportsmanship include shaking hands with opponents before and after a game, acknowledging when someone else plays well and accepting bad calls gracefully.

My goal is to:
Play Nicely with Someone

Playing nicely can cover a range of behaviours. Encourage children to share appropriately, take turns when playing games or using toys and show self-control when they are feeling angry or frustrated. Children may disagree with the best way to play, but try to help them resolve disagreements appropriately, without tantrums, hitting or throwing.

My goal is to:
Dress Myself

Teaching kids to dress themselves can take patience, especially during the morning rush. However, your patience will be rewarded when you see them develop their sense of independence and watch their thinking and their motor skills improve. So, try and be there to help them get dressed, without doing it for them. They're also developing their own taste and fashion preferences, and may enjoy picking out their own clothes for themselves. If this process takes too long, select three outfits and allow your child to choose from them instead of choosing something from their entire wardrobe.

Eating, Sleeping and Healthy Self-care

Building good self-care skills is important, as it encourages independence and feelings of self-worth, and establishes beneficial habits that will last a lifetime. Implementing a routine can be hard in the short-term, but it will pay off in the long term. Children are happier, more positive and better behaved when they know and understand what to expect. You must be dedicated to establishing, enforcing and reinforcing the routine. Mealtime and bedtime are key areas to develop healthy routines for.

Mealtimes

Mealtimes should be happy times where families enjoy sharing nutritious foods. However, they can be one of the biggest causes of conflict over behaviour. Decide what time you want your child and family to eat; there should be little variance between weekdays and weekends.

Eating together as a family helps maintain good eating behaviour and manners. If your child is old enough, involve them in creating the routine: setting the table, packing away, washing up, etc. They can help choose and prepare the meal, which increases the chance that they'll eat it and can help fussy eaters try new foods. Reasonable expectations for your child's table behaviour can help eliminate mealtime battles. Turn off the TV and other screens and remove toys from the table.

Try new foods when your child is relaxed and isn't tired. Offer new foods alongside foods that your child already likes. Have realistic expectations: ask your child to try everything on the plate or take a certain number of mouthfuls. It can take several tries for children to accept and enjoy new foods. If your child refuses, offer it again in a week or so.

Bedtime

Bedtime can be one of the biggest causes of conflict and emotional turmoil. The first step is to decide what time you want your child to go to bed. Work back from then to allow enough time for your child to complete their bedtime routine. Make sure that they understand that the routine must be performed in a timely manner with no fuss. If they drag their feet, story time will be shorter, because lights-out time never changes.

Goals

These goals are designed to encourage children to improve their eating, sleeping, hygiene and healthy self-care skills. The ten goals in this section are included on the goals stickers and are appropriate for a wide range of ages.

Wash and Brush My Hair

Teaching good hygiene goes a long way towards keeping your kids healthy. Plus, caring appropriately about their appearance will help build self-esteem. To wash a child's hair, try to use a mild shampoo that doesn't sting their eyes. When they are old enough, teach them how to shampoo and rinse their own hair. Encourage your child to brush their own hair.

Go to Bed on Time

Sleep is crucial to your child's health, growth and development. Children perform better and are much happier when they've had more sleep. But getting the kids to go to bed on time can often be the source of serious negotiations. Keeping a routine and a regular bedtime is one of the best ways to ensure good sleeping habits. Having a cue, like reading a book, will help your child understand that it is time for bed and help them wind down and get ready for a good night's sleep.

Eat Fresh Fruit and Vegetables

While not always popular with children, vegetables provide vitamins, minerals and fibre. It is recommended your child eat at least one serve of vegetables as part of each main meal. Try to choose a variety of vegetables of assorted colours and textures. Putting vegetables in a stir fry, casserole or bolognaise sauce will help give your child their daily requirements without causing too much fuss.

As well as being a great sweet, fruit provides vitamins, minerals and fibre. Offer at least one serve of fruit every day as a snack or for a second course. Adding a banana, berries or a pear to a child's cereal is a great way to include fruit in their diet. A smoothie made from real fruit is another smart idea, and frozen bananas and grapes are a clever snack idea for summer.

Use the Toilet

Starting to use the toilet is an important step in a younger child's life. Some children get the knack quickly, while others need more patience and support. If your child is having trouble, it may be best to delay the process for a few months. And of course, loads of verbal encouragement is key.

Be Sun Smart

It's always important to be sun smart, especially if you live in a hot climate. Keep the following in mind to ensure your child is protected.

- Wear appropriate protective clothing. Long sleeves and a high collar will protect the neck and help prevent sun damage.
- Use a high SPF broad-spectrum sunscreen. Remember to reapply frequently, especially after swimming or physical activity.
- Wear a hat that provides appropriate cover, including the neck.
- Seek shade, especially in the middle of the day between 10am and 3pm when UV radiation is most intense. If possible, use a portable shade-shelter or beach umbrella.
- Wear quality kid-sized sunglasses. Find a reputable brand that makes good-quality lenses to ensure children's eyes don't get damaged.

Children don't always like putting on sunscreen so look for products with trouble-free application options, such as a spray or roll-on. Demonstrate good sun-safe behaviours yourself too. Creating good habits when children are young can help prevent sun damage later in life and even save them from developing melanomas or skin cancers.

Choose Healthy Snacks

Deciding what types of snacks to serve your children is important when planning your child's overall diet. We all need a snack now and then. The challenge is making sure your child has a snack that delivers nutrition. Kids need regular opportunities to stock up on enough nutrients throughout the day. Some good snacks include bread, cereals, fruit, veggies and milk-based drinks. It can help to prepare healthy snacks in advance: try cutting up fruit and veggies in containers in the fridge so your children are more likely to choose them when hunger strikes. Snacks can also be a fantastic way to get your child to eat more fruit and vegetables.

Have a Bath or Shower

It's important to teach kids good bathing techniques. A daily bath or shower is great, especially on hot days when they are sweaty or have sunscreen on their skin. Teach them how to correctly wash all the parts of their body. Toys can help make the bath more fun, and if your child thinks they are too old or grown up for a bath, try a shower instead. Remember, do not leave young children unattended in the bath.

Try a New Food

It's important to try new foods. Just because your child has rejected a food once, it doesn't mean you should stop offering it. The more often a new food is offered, the more likely it is to be accepted. Try not to make a fuss about a new food, as this often makes things worse, and offer the new food accompanied by other, more familiar foods.

Brush My Teeth

Try to teach your child to brush their teeth when they're about two years of age. Starting early will help them develop a good routine. You should help them brush until they are old enough to do it properly for themselves. They should be brushing their teeth twice a day, after breakfast and before going to bed. It's best to use a small toothbrush with soft bristles designed specifically for younger children and a pea-sized amount of low-fluoride children's toothpaste.

Wash My Hands

Help your child develop good hygiene habits as early as possible. Something as simple as washing their hands will go a long way to protecting them against illness. You need to teach your child to wash their hands by using clean water and soap, and drying off with a clean towel. Also teach them to wash before preparing food and eating, after they go to the toilet, after playing with animals, after being around sick people or after blowing their nose.

Suggestions for Blank Goal Stickers

Here are some ideas for further healthy self-care goals that you can write on to the blank goal stickers. These suggestions cover a range of themes. Choose an area your feel your child could work on. Feel free to add your own ideas for goals on the blank goal stickers too.

> My goal is to:
> Eat a Healthy Breakfast

Eating a good breakfast is important for everyone. Skipping the first meal of the day causes many people to underperform and can even contribute to weight gain. Porridge, baked beans on toast, fruit and yoghurt, fortified cereal or wholemeal toast are all good ways to start the day.

> My goal is to:
> Eat a Healthy Lunch

We all know how difficult it is to find a food that gives your child the nutrition they need while also being something they would consider eating. Filling a sandwich or pita bread with egg and lettuce, tuna and corn, cheese or even a mashed banana are all good lunch ideas.

> My goal is to:
> Eat a Healthy Dinner

When thinking about what to make for dinner, try to choose food from the five food groups. It might be useful to write down some quick and easy recipes for reference when life gets hectic. Try to make dinnertime fun, and make sure that children haven't filled up on snacks or treats before they sit down to eat.

> My goal is to: Choose Healthy
> Food from the Canteen

Eating from the school canteen or tuckshop should be done occasionally: once a week or as a treat. By the time children can choose and purchase food for themselves, they'll be getting all sorts of unhealthy food messages from friends and advertising. Start teaching them about healthy foods while they are young. If possible, send kids to school with a healthy packed lunch instead.

> **My goal is to:**
> Drink Water

Water is essential for keeping little bodies running well. After a young child has stopped breastfeeding, parents should offer water and cow's milk as the main drinks. If you do offer juice, limit it to just every now and then, and dilute its high sugar content by adding water.

> **My goal is to:**
> Cover My Mouth When I Cough

Teach your child to protect themselves and others against illness by covering their mouths when they cough or sneeze. If they are unwell, they should be taught to wash their hands regularly as well as clean things they have touched to stop making others sick.

> **My goal is to:**
> Be Brave at the Doctor

Going to the doctor can be a scary prospect for most children. If your child gets nervous, help them by clearly explaining what they can expect and what is going to happen. For example: 'We are going to the doctor because you have an earache. The doctor is going to look inside your ear with a light and suggest some things to make it better.' It's a good idea to establish a good relationship with a regular family doctor so your children become familiar with them and trust them.

> **My goal is to:**
> Visit the Dentist

We all know brushing our teeth is important, but we also need to visit the dentist regularly to maintain good oral and dental health. Explain to your child that during the visit, the dentist will look at their teeth and gums to check for any problems and to make sure little teeth are developing properly. Seeing the dentist every six months is ideal. It can be reassuring to have your own dental check-up at the same time, so your child can see what happens and that you are OK.

> **My goal is to:**
> Use a Tissue to Blow my Nose

Some children are happy to run around with a runny nose, or to sniff their way through the day. However, it's important that they use a tissue, especially when sick, as that prevents the spread of germs. Young children may need assistance when learning how to blow their nose. Use bath time to show them how to blow air out their nose, reminding them to keep their mouth closed. They should also learn that they must throw away a used tissue.

> **My goal is to:**
> Sleep All Night

Getting your child to stay in bed until morning can be the cause of a huge amount of frustration and exhaustion. Whether it's getting out of bed after you have said good night or constantly waking during the night, help your child by developing soothing, regular and enforced bedtime routines.

Rewards Guide

Reward stickers give your child an end goal to work towards. A reward can be chosen once your child has received seven motivational stickers, or you can select the reward before your child even starts, to add extra incentive.

Reward stickers

The 20 rewards listed here feature on the stickers provided. They are designed to be inexpensive and fun for the whole family.

Extra Kisses and Cuddles

Kisses and cuddles are simple and inexpensive ways to make children feel loved. Children need love and attention from their parents to grow into happy and healthy adults. We should cherish and savour these moments because children grow up so fast they won't always let us do this to them. Find something special to say about your children when you are giving them kisses and cuddles.

Fun Physical Activity

Choose any form of physical activity that is both fun and beneficial. Some fun activities you might want to think about include flying a kite, riding bikes along the river, splashing about at the local pool, throwing a frisbee, roller-skating, chasing bubbles, jumping on a trampoline or putting on a pair of gumboots and going puddle-jumping.

Family Picnic

Children love finger food, fresh air, games and freedom from table manners. It's a great escape from your normal routine, and gives you a perfect opportunity to spend some quality family time in the great outdoors. Don't limit yourself to parks with playgrounds. Why not try the local pool or have it in your own backyard? Invite friends to bring along their own picnics, and you've got a party!

Pocket Money

Giving pocket money will help your child understand the value of money, especially if they have to work for it. The amount of money doesn't matter. Pocket money helps teach kids about saving, waiting for things they want and spending thoughtfully.

Fun Arty, Crafty Activity

Kids love to be busy making all sorts of things. Keep a craft-and-activity bag or box full of scraps of paper, stickers, stencils, glue, glitter and other crafty items for them to play with as a reward. One idea is to cut out the outline of a house using coloured plain paper, then cut an assortment of shapes such as windows, doors, trees, people and pets. Use washable non-toxic markers or crayons to draw more details like bricks, a kitchen or a garden. Let your child place or glue the shapes onto the house. You can also play make-believe and talk about what happens in this house.

Fun Musical Activity

What child doesn't like making noise? Use instruments to play along to songs on the radio or on a music player. If you don't have any instruments, one idea is to collect some items from around the house that would make a different noise when shaken around inside a plastic container. You could use rice, sugar, sand or water. Put each item into an opaque container. Let your child shake the containers and guess what's in each one. Then play your new instrument along to a song!

Extra Story at Bedtime

Children often want one more story at bedtime. Now you can say YES! And to make the reward extra special, visit the library or bookshop and let children choose some special books. This will give them the chance to see other little readers enjoying themselves, too. Look for titles that reflect your child's everyday experiences and pull out several books at a time and let your child pick their own. They will love being involved in the decision.

Play at the Park

Free play at a park of choice is always a winner. It has so many benefits, including allowing children to use their creativity while developing their imagination, dexterity and physical, cognitive and emotional skills. Try different types of parks for different experiences: for example, sand parks, water parks, nature parks, etc.

Special Time with a Person of my Choice

Kids love spending time with grandparents, aunts, uncles, cousins and special friends. So, let them choose who they want to have quality time with. You can even make a day of it with a special meal or outing.

Visit the Library

Most libraries are child friendly. Many have free story readings or nursery-rhyme times, as well as a cosy corner where kids can lounge on beanbags or sit on kid-sized chairs while they read. During holidays, many libraries put on free shows, arts-and-crafts activities or other kid-friendly programs.

Ride on a Train, Bus, Tram or Ferry

Travelling by public transport can be very exciting for children. Encourage the kids to bring a camera to take pictures of their journey and make a journal or travel diary. Bring along a sketch pad and a box of crayons or markers. For each event along the way, have your child draw a picture of what they saw and did that day, and write about it. You can also paste in souvenirs such as brochures and other mementos.

Mystery Surprise

Kids love surprises. One idea is to fill a small photo album with photos of a recent holiday or time spent with a friend. Another is to decorate a brown paper bag with stickers and fill it with some fun small items from your child's favourite toy store.

Buy Seeds to Sprout

It's exciting to plant a seed and watch it grow. Most kids like to watch plants grow, especially if they grow quickly. Mung beans begin to sprout in 48 hours in a screw-top jar of water, and they are edible in a week. Alfalfa seeds are easy to grow and can be bought at a health-food store. Avocado pips can also yield quick results, and then they can be planted in the garden for longer-term results. Once planted in the ground, tomato seeds quickly grow into sweet, delicious fruit that your kids can pick and eat.

My Favourite Dinner

Make dinner fun by turning your kitchen or dining room into a restaurant. Each child can have one night to choose the food and to decide how to decorate the dining room. Kids can design and draw up a menu. You could even create two or more dishes and take everyone's order, like in a restaurant. The other meal can be saved for lunch the next day.

Sleepover

Slumber parties are a fun tradition and a rite of passage when growing up. Let the kids think of some fun games like a backyard treasure hunt, hair-styling sessions, basketball or soccer. Physical activities are particularly good if you want to tire them out a little in the hope they won't be up all night! You could also make a video of the event.

Go on a Play Date

Playing with friends is so much fun for children and an easy reward to fulfil. Let your child decide who they would like to invite over and what creative activities they could do together. Talk about the importance of making guests feel welcome. For the very little ones, it might be a good idea to hide any favourite toys to avoid any arguments until they are old enough to fully understand sharing.

Go for a Bike Ride

This is a great activity that the entire family can enjoy together. If your children are too small to ride themselves, consider using child seats or attachments. Choose a safe location with bike paths, away from busy roads. Exercising together also sends the right message of the importance of physical health to kids.

Trip to the Movies

Taking your children to the movies is a great family outing that everyone will enjoy. Daytime movies are usually a great option for families with kids. Make sure you check the movie rating before you go to ensure it's an appropriate film to see. It's also a good idea to remind your kids not to speak or run around during the movie. Some movie theatres have kid-friendly cinemas or movie sessions too.

Family Day Out

A family day out is a great way to enjoy some special time together. Life can get so busy, it often leaves us little time for our families. An outing is a reward everyone will enjoy. During the planning stage, let your kids suggest a venue or occasion and let them contribute by giving them fun tasks such as taking pictures or choosing the food.

Fun Get-Messy Activity

Kids love making a mess, especially when it's done with your consent. One idea is to put out a large sheet of butcher's paper on the lawn or hang it from the clothesline. Then pour several colours of water-based paint onto plastic plates. Let your child smear their hands in the paint and enjoy some finger painting. If it's a warm day, they can wear an old top and use their whole arm.

Suggestions for Blank Reward Stickers

This section includes some suggested rewards you could use to fill in the customisable blank reward stickers. Use these ideas or get inspired by them to create your own rewards! Write them on the blank stickers and stick them on the reward chart. You can also ask your child to come up with their own ideas for the blank reward stickers.

> My reward is to:
> Visit a Museum or Art Gallery

Some galleries and museums are free and have fabulous facilities or programs for kids. School holidays are a particularly good time to visit as they often put on child-friendly workshops and exhibitions.

> My reward is to:
> Visit the Local Fire Brigade

Many young children have a strong interest in firefighters and fire trucks. A special outing can be a great awareness exercise and an exciting adventure for children. A visit to a local station can also be a good opportunity to remind kids how to avoid burns and what to do if one should occur. Many fire stations hold firefighting and safety displays at regular times.

> My reward is a:
> Backyard Campout

Camping in your backyard is loads of fun, whatever your age. It's great for keeping the kids entertained, for offering opportunities to check out the night sky and to stargaze, and for spending quality time together as a family. It's also a great way to have a break from your everyday routine. Just check the weather forecast before setting up!

> My reward is:
> Something at the Supermarket

Help children choose one or two of their favourite nutrient-rich snacks. Engage them in selecting and purchasing food at farmers' markets or in the family garden. Let them find a 'new food of the week' to expand their horizons. Shopping for food can also become a learning experience.

My reward is a:
Family Movie Night

Here are some ways to make a movie night even more fun. Ask your children to make tickets and get them to sell them at a 'box office' (a large cardboard box that's cut out and decorated to look like a real box office). They can even 'usher' their parents to their seats, using a small torch. They can make theatre scenery out of another big box. Beanbag chairs and large pillows on the floor are great movie seats. Everyone will also enjoy snacks like popcorn, pretzels, homemade ice-cream and healthy treats.

My reward is to:
Explore Nature

Most children are fascinated by the wonders of nature. Taking them on a nature walk is a great adventure. You can start in your own backyard and then venture to a park or beach. Inspect every leaf, twig, insect and rock. You can look up the names of things on the internet as you go too.

Top Parenting Tips to Remember

At times, parenting can be challenging work. Use the parenting strategies in this book and make use of tools such as the reward chart and stickers, which will help you navigate some of these challenges. Above all, keep in mind these handy parenting tips.

- Children learn best by copying: as a parent, you need to model best behaviour, including manners, kindness and courtesy, for your child to copy.

- Do the best you can with the information you have available at the time.

- Everybody else thinks they are an expert on parenting and can always be relied on to tell you what you are doing wrong! Trust your own judgement.

- Be flexible and adaptable – do whatever works for you and your family!

Remember, as the famous quote says,

For things to change,
first I must change.